THIS CANDLEWICK BOOK BELONGS TO:

FOR ABEL
May you see well and hear happily!

CANDLEWICK PRESS

In the beginning, there was only
the deep,
dark

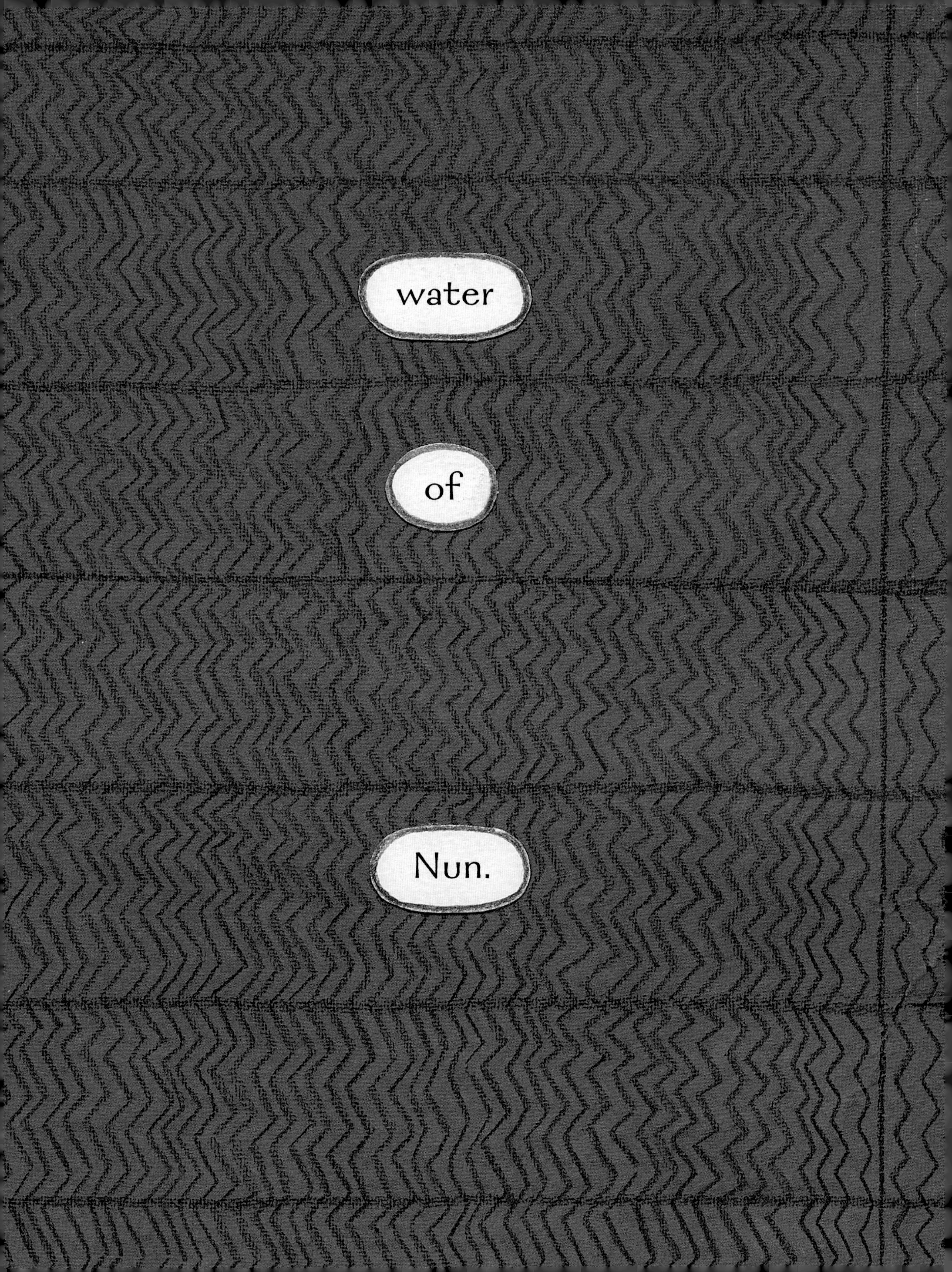
water
of
Nun.

Then out of the water rose an island.
On the island stood Ra, the Shining One.
Ra was the first god to stand on the land of Egypt.

Ra had a secret name, which gave him the power to bring anything into being with just a word or a glance!
Shu
Tefnut
First Ra brought forth Shu, the god of air, and Tefnut, the goddess of rain.
Then came Geb, the god of the earth, and Nut, the goddess of the sky.
Then Ra named Hapi, the great river Nile that flows through Egypt.
Welcome!
After this Ra gave life to men and women and all the things on Earth, both great and small.
Am I your favorite?
We'll see.
Then Ra took on the shape of a man and became the first Pharaoh of Egypt. And every year the river Nile rose up and flooded the fields to help the crops grow. So there was peace and plenty in the reign of Ra.
And the cat named Rami was Ra's favorite. And to him Ra gave many lives!

ISIS AND THE COBRA
If we marry, I'll be your queen!
Good plan. Keep it in the family!
In the reign of Ra, Nut and Geb gave birth to the clever goddess Isis. She married her brother Osiris, the likely heir to Ra's crown.
Yuck, he's drooling.
As time passed, Ra's human form grew old.
I like being pharaoh!
Not for long. It's our turn.
Yet he still did not want to give Osiris his crown.
I'll find out his secret name!
So Isis used her magic powers against him.
You will carry the venom of darkness!
When Ra drooled on the ground, Isis formed the damp sand into a cobra.
I don't remember creating you.
The next day, the light of Ra's eye fell on the serpent and gave it life!

Well, you'll remember my bite!
The cobra reared up and bit Ra, who cried out in agony.
Sorry, only Isis can help you.
Isn't there one god who can help me?
The pain grew like fire in Ra's limbs, and his eyes slowly dimmed.
If I mix your secret name with my magic, I can cure you.
I am Khepera in the dawn,
Ra at noon,
and Tum in the evening.
Isis offered to heal him if he told her his secret name. Ra spoke many names, but not his name of power.
Ha, so that's it!
Get your own crown, Osiris.
Finally, the pain grew unbearable and Ra let his secret name pass to Isis. Isis bade the serpent's venom leave him, and Ra was at peace.

Where are the fish?
Once he had shared his secret name with Isis, Ra could no longer reign on Earth.
He took his place in the heavens and traveled across the sky in the likeness of the sun.
He became known as Amen Ra.
Behave, or it's back to the Duat!
Sorry, Ra, but I'm off to live my nine lives on Earth.
At night he passed through the underworld, called the Duat. As dawn rose he returned to the heavens, taking with him the spirits of the dead who had won a place in his heavenly kingdom.
Splash . . .
and into the river Nile!
One life gone, but I'm back in the land of the living.
I need to teach Ra's creatures to respect cats!
I'm here to tell you a few of ancient Egypt's top secrets.

The above activities are recommended by our great pharaoh, Osiris, and his queen.
It's best not to eat one another.
But the lion ate my rabbit, O Pharaoh.
On Earth, Osiris became Pharaoh of Egypt, and Isis became his queen. They cared well for their people, teaching them many things — including not to eat one another. They also built a great temple for Amen Ra in their new city of Thebes.
In Egypt cats eat ducks — ducks don't eat cats!
Nile crocodiles are dangerous!
The Egyptian people fear them.
Crocs eat anything — even cats.
Burp!
Meow, another life gone, seven to go.

SETH THE EVIL ONE
Life, health, and power.
O beloved Pharaoh.
Death, sickness, and weakness, O unbeloved Pharaoh.
Everyone loved Pharaoh Osiris — except his younger brother, Seth. He wanted to be pharaoh and planned to steal Osiris's crown.
Excellent banquet!
It gets better!
Seth invited Osiris to a banquet with some of Seth's wicked friends. After the feasting a casket was carried in — a gift from Seth to anyone who fit inside it!
After cats, the wisest of Ra's creatures is mankind.
Soon after their creation, they decide to take up farming.
They grow crops along the banks of the Nile.
Wheat
Barley
Figs
Pomegranates
Grapes
Vegetables

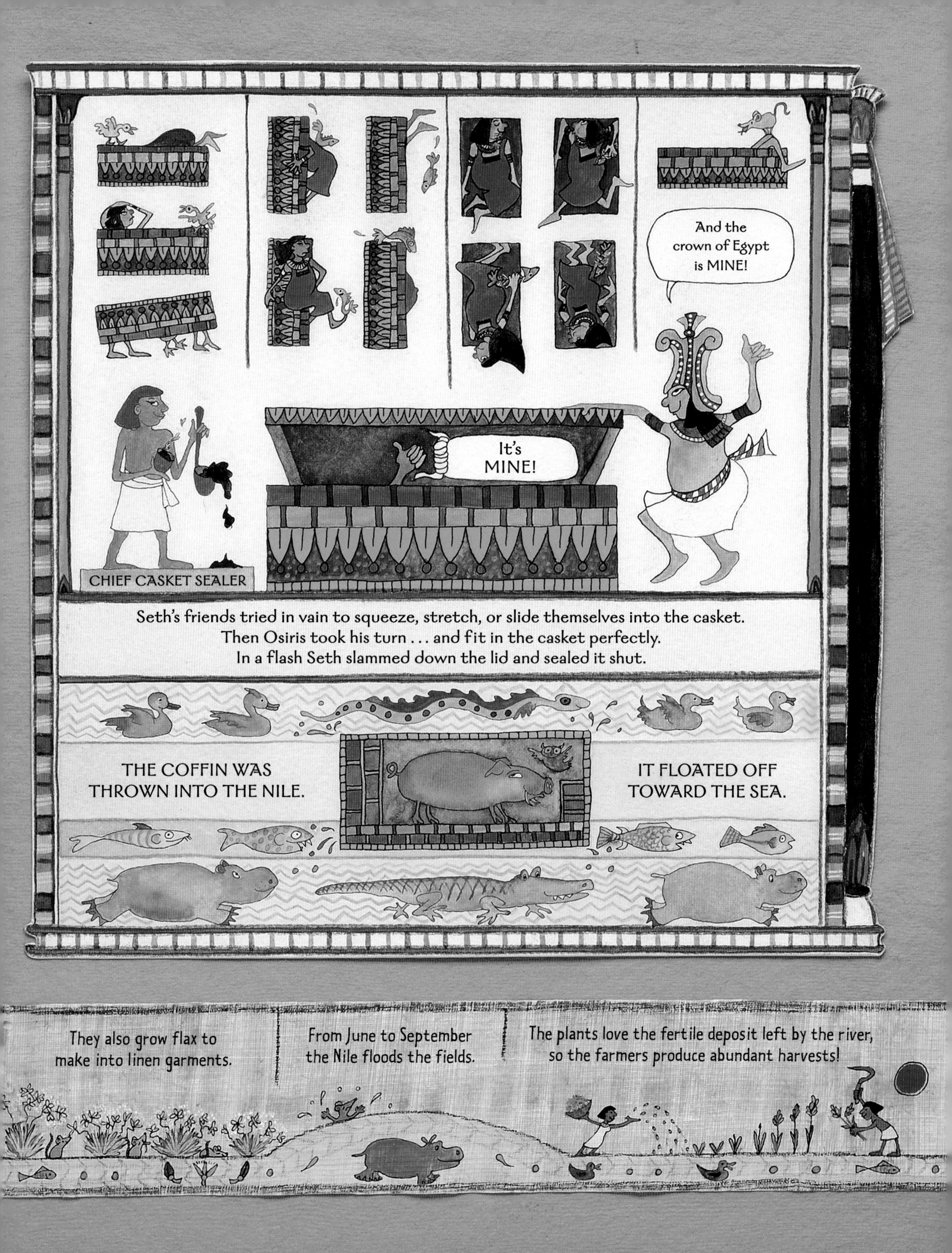
And the crown of Egypt is MINE!
It's MINE!
CHIEF CASKET SEALER
Seth's friends tried in vain to squeeze, stretch, or slide themselves into the casket.
Then Osiris took his turn . . . and fit in the casket perfectly.
In a flash Seth slammed down the lid and sealed it shut.
THE COFFIN WAS THROWN INTO THE NILE.
IT FLOATED OFF TOWARD THE SEA.
They also grow flax to make into linen garments.
From June to September the Nile floods the fields.
The plants love the fertile deposit left by the river, so the farmers produce abundant harvests!

How will he pass to the underworld if I don't find his body?
Waaah!
Queen Isis was heartbroken at the loss of her husband.
Keep him hidden from his uncle Seth!
Leaving their baby son, Horus, behind, she set out to find Osiris's body.
No wonder this Tamarisk smells so sweet.
After many weeks Isis reached the city of Byblos where, with the help of her magic, she discovered Osiris's coffin.
Just stay hidden while I prepare your tomb.
Have you come back to haunt me?
Isis hurried back to Egypt, but before she could place Osiris in his tomb, Seth found his body.
Now try haunting me!
He chopped his brother's body into fourteen pieces and scattered them across the land of Egypt.

Animals help the farmers plow and carry loads.
Some animals provide food.
Cows
Goats
Pigs
Geese
Ducks
Meat
Eggs
Milk
Cheese

Poor, brave Isis set out once more to search for her husband's body.
There's still a piece missing!
Burp!
After weeks of searching she found all but one part of Osiris's body.
Isis conjured a whole body in each place!
To protect Osiris from Seth, Isis buried Osiris in thirteen different places!
I will have my revenge!
So finally, the spirit of Osiris passed into the Duat, where he became King of the Dead . . .
Now that I'm a pharaoh as well as a god I can be twice as EVIL!
while his wicked brother, Seth, became Pharaoh of Egypt, which was more than he deserved!
Wild cats keep the rats and mice from the grain stores.
Cats soon become tame.
They are ancient Egypt's favorite pet — no home is complete without one . . . or two!

HORUS THE AVENGER!
We don't want that nasty Horus stealing you, do we?
Seth was Pharaoh of Egypt, but the crown really belonged to his nephew, Horus.
We'll just have to kill him, won't we, my precious?
Seth decided to kill him, as he'd killed Osiris, Horus's father.
You are safe from your nasty uncle Seth here.
I wouldn't bet on it.
Horus was still a child and guarded by his mother, Isis, on a floating island.
One night, as the island bumped against the banks of the Nile, Seth crossed onto it.
He took the shape of a scorpion and crawled into Horus's room, where he stung him.
A cat is often taken hunting instead of dogs — MEOW!
A cat is better at retrieving ducks and fish from the marshes.
Before long the ancient Egyptians had made the cat a god!
The most famous cat goddess is Bastet.

My magic has no power against such evil.
All night Horus screamed as Isis tried to heal him, but by morning he appeared dead.
He is the rightful pharaoh; he will live again.
The wise god Thoth comforted Isis and reassured her that she would see her son again.
You will avenge us.
Do not doubt it, Dad.
Horus had passed into the Duat, but only so that his father, Osiris, could prepare him to fight Seth and avenge their deaths.
Never doubt Seth's power.
I am ready for anything Seth can throw at me!
Horus remained with Osiris until he became a man and was ready to meet Seth in battle.
Or Bast, as she is known when she takes the body of a woman.
Bastet is the goddess of fertility and the protector of children.
The temples of Bastet are full of pampered cats.
Warning! You can be put to death for killing a CAT!
Strangle him!
Meow!

You may need more than weapons to fight Seth.
I do have some magic powers.
Amen Ra took Horus to the land of the living in his sacred boat.
It's Seth!
Seth was ready and waiting. He charged at Horus and aimed a bolt of fire into his eyes.
He's blinded me.
I'll heal you.
Horus was blinded and unable to fight back. He roared with pain and anger.
REST
DARK
HERBS
WALKS
RETURN TO BATTLE
Run!
It was many weeks before Horus regained his sight and could go after Seth again.
Sekhmet is also a cat goddess.
She is a lion and is fiercer than Bastet.
ROAR!
Sekhmet protects the pharaohs.
She expects large offerings — or else!

Got you!
Got you!
Got you!
Got you!
I need an army!
Every time Horus thought he had his enemy cornered, the wily Seth escaped.
Come on, guys, he's out there somewhere.
So Horus gathered a great army and chased Seth up the river Nile.
Let there come a raging tempest and a mighty flood against my enemies!
When they reached the island of Elephantine, Horus saw Seth standing there in the form of a vast red hippopotamus, uttering a terrible curse.

Miw is the ancient Egyptian word for "cat."
Here, miw.
When a pet cat dies the family shaves off their eyebrows.
Eyebrows, not hair.
They also howl a lot to show their grief!
HOWL!
They may even have their feline friend mummified!

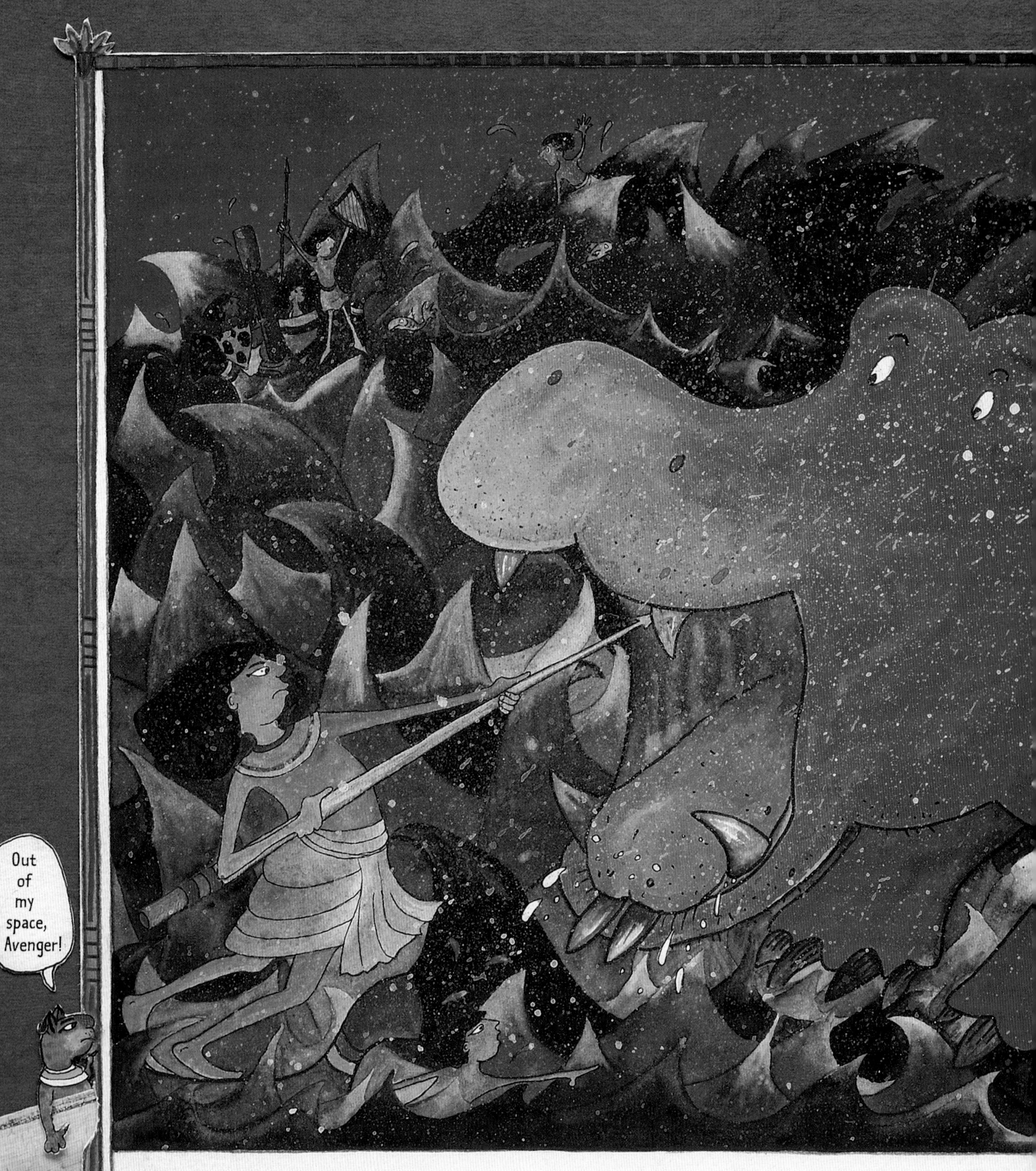

The wind raged, the waves rose, and blackness fell over Egypt.
Only the boat of Horus gleamed in the darkness as the gigantic hippopotamus opened its jaws to crush him. Quickly, Horus took the likeness of a giant youth.
He drew back his arm and cast a long harpoon.

Horus threw it with such force that it traveled through the roof of Seth's mouth and into his brain. The red hippopotamus sank dead into the Nile, the darkness vanished, and the people of Egypt rejoiced at the victory of Horus the Avenger.
Peace came to Egypt, and Horus was crowned pharaoh.

Inside, wonderful etchings and carvings decorated the walls leading to Zoser's burial chamber. Never before had such a large stone monument been built, not even for the great god Ra, creator of all Egypt. For as long as it stood, Pharaoh Zoser would be remembered, which made him very, very happy.

Will it last?
Until the end of time.
Ra's :hosen one is not eceiving proper espect.
Even Pharaoh Zoser was satisfied with his tomb! It was a beautiful step pyramid built at Saqqara, on the edge of the desert. The outside was covered in white limestone that glinted in the sunlight. At night it looked like a stairway to the heavens.

PHARAOH ZOSER AND THE GREAT FAMINE
Scribe, change that to: GREAT PHARAOH ZOSER AND THE FAMINE!
It's time you all retired to the heavens.
O Ra, we thought you'd never let us!
After the reign of Horus, the great gods decided to leave the day-to-day ruling of Egypt to mortals.
Am I the greatest?
You are great.
You are very great.
You are very, very, great.
But there is no way you are as great as Ra and the other ancient gods.
One of the first of these pharaohs was Zoser. Like other mortal pharaohs he was worshipped as a god, but everyone knew that the ancient gods came first.
Build me a tomb that rises higher than any temple to the ancient gods.
O Pharaoh, I love a challenge!
So pharaoh Zoser shouldn't have asked his adviser, Imhotep, to build him a tomb greater than any temple in Egypt.
Is my tomb never to be ready?
O Pharaoh, come, it awaits you.
Imhotep could not disobey his pharaoh, and eventually, he declared that Zoser's burial place was ready.
OPEN
That hippo has used up at least four of my lives.
While I recover, I'll tell you about some of Egypt's fantastic inventions.
C. 3500 BC: Senet — the world's first known board game
C. 3200 BC: Hieroglyphs — a form of writing, first used in wall paintings.
Rami walks in the rai

Wow! Pharaoh Zoser is the best!
The people of Egypt came to admire Zoser's magnificent pyramid and to praise the pharaoh who had ordered it to be built.
Come, help me repair the mighty temple of Thoth.
Sorry, we're off to worship at Zoser's tomb.
Meanwhile, the old gods were being neglected, and their temples were crumbling.
You are sowing seeds in desert land.
Well, it's ALL desert land!
Then one year the Nile did not rise as usual, and the land became infertile.
Just one each.
Next year the Nile is bound to rise!
The crops failed, and the people of Egypt had to live on the grain stored from other years.
C.3000 BC: Papyrus — used to write on and made from the papyrus plant!
C.2700 BC: Pyramids — Zoser's step pyramid was the first!
Still not quite myself, so I'll hand over the next page to Desheri, an embalmer!

Go back; the store houses are empty.
The next year the Nile failed to rise again, but now the stores of grain were empty.
Health to you, O Pharaoh. Your people need food.
The Nile will not obey my divine powers.
The people turned to Zoser for help, but he did not have the power to raise the waters of the Nile.
Dear gods, please help us . . . please!
Did we hear a prayer? No, we think not.
At last, Zoser appealed to the gods, but they were angry with him and ignored his pleas.
For seven years the Nile failed to flood. Farmland turned to desert, and the Egyptians starved.
I'll eat the rat or I'll eat you!
Help!
You're our pharaoh; DO SOMETHING!
Neighbor robbed neighbor, children were left to die, and fists were raised at Zoser.

Embalmers turn dead bodies into mummies! By about 2700 BC we were excellent embalmers!
IN JUST SEVENTY DAYS YOU CAN TRAVEL TO THE NEXT LIFE AS A MUMMY!
1 Stick a hook up the nostrils and pull out the brain. Feed it to the fish.
2 Slice open the body, remove the organs, and store them in canopic jars.
Gulp!

Find out which god directs the flood ... and hurry!
I'll try, but I'm weak with hunger.
Zoser ordered Imhotep to go to Thebes and consult with Thoth, the god of wisdom.
I bring you gifts and apologies.
Only Khnemu has power over the Nile.
Thoth told Imhotep that Zoser must travel to Elephantine and pray to the god Khnemu.
I am but a grain of sand compared to the great god Khnemu.
Once more and then I'll forgive you!
So Zoser took the royal barge to the island of Elephantine. He prayed to Khnemu to be forgiven for neglecting the gods. He ordered a temple grander even than his tomb to be built for Khnemu. This pleased Khnemu, and he called for the Nile to rise over the land so that the crops would flourish and the famine would end. Once more Egypt became a land of plenty, but Zoser never again risked neglecting the ancient gods!
3 Cover the body with salt and leave to dry for forty days.
4 Stuff the body with sweet herbs and spices.
5 Wrap the body in bandages.
6 Put a mask over the mummy's face so you know who it is.
Yes, we do cats, too!
Meow!

Amen Ra, the king of the gods, looked down on Egypt
and decided it was time she was ruled by a queen.
He chose Ahmes, wife of Pharaoh Thutmose, to be the queen's mother.

Enough of death.
There's life in the old cat yet!
I'll tell you about those
tail-tweaking things called CHILDREN!
As well as tails, they play with mud,
sand, sticks, and stones.

Amen Ra and Thoth went to the palace of Thutmose
and cast a spell upon the household so that every living thing slept.
Then Ra entered the chamber of Ahmes, bathing the room in light.
As he placed himself beside her, the couch rose up so that it was neither on the earth nor in the heavens.
Ra held a sweet perfume to Ahmes's nostrils, and the breath of life passed into her.
ome children may have tops, dolls,
toy weapons, and the
odd pull-along animal.
Swimming is also popular...
especially with the crocodiles.
Help!
Ball games, wrestling, racing,
and dancing are all good fun!

After nine months, a baby girl named Hatshepsut was born to Ahmes. All of Egypt rejoiced.
Once again a great sleep fell upon the palace while Ra visited the child.
He took with him Hathor, the goddess of love, and her seven daughters, who weave the web of life for all newborns. Ra gave Hatshepsut the kiss of power, while the Hathors wove the golden web of her life so that she would be a great queen. And all the while the palace slept.
School is not so popular!
A boy's ears are in his backside.
But if you want to grow up to be a scribe, doctor, lawyer, priest, or adviser you have to go.
We don't even want to grow up!
Most girls are educated at home. Not many learn to read or write. Some girls become dancers, singers, or musicians; only a few become scribes.

Be kind to your people.
Be fair to your people.
Be generous to your people.
As Hatshepsut grew, she took her place beside her earthly father, Pharaoh Thutmose, and learned how to care for his people.
Let the birds fly across the land telling the people that I'm their new pharaoh!
That's my GIRL!
Then the time came for Hatshepsut to be crowned Pharaoh of all Egypt.
Hatshepsut and Amen Ra were both very happy, for they had always known that this was her destiny.
Pharaoh Hatshepsut was a wise and powerful ruler, and Egypt flourished under the rule of its queen!
The ancient Egyptians marry young, so childhood is short.
Soon children become parents.
It is the duty of children to honor and look after their parents . . . and their pet CATS!

PRINCE THUTMOSE AND THE SPHINX
The start of Pharaoh Hatshepsut's journey to the next life.
After the death of Queen Hatshepsut, her stepson Thutmose became pharaoh, followed by his grandson Amenhotep.
My best boy!
Pharaoh Amenhotep had many sons, but his favorite was named Thutmose, after his grandfather.
Daddy's boy!
Daddy's boy!
The other brothers were jealous of Thutmose and didn't want him to inherit the crown.
Thutmose broke your crown!
Thutmose ate your supper!
Thutmose squashed your cat!
They were often unkind and tried hard to turn their father against him.
Thutmose would escape from their taunts by going hunting.

Cats are Egypt's greatest wonder, followed by the river Nile.
It gives us many gifts and even carries the stones used for pyramid building.
It also provides the water for the people who help to build the pyramids.
They live in villages that are settled close to the building sites.

One day, when the court was at Memphis for a festival, Thutmose and two companions left to hunt gazelles in the desert. They rode until midday, when the heat forced them to stop and rest.
Unable to forget his brothers' jealousy, Thutmose was too unhappy to rest.
He decided to leave his sleeping companions and explore the great pyramids of Giza.

Secret rooms are hidden deep inside the pyramids to keep out tomb raiders.
False chamber
Warning statues of gods and sphinxes are built outside the pyramids.
Roar!
Nice kitty.
Some robbers still plunder the treasure meant for the pharaoh in his next life.
I'm rich!
May they grow rat tails, mouse whiskers, and fish scales!
I'm transformed.

If he doesn't get out of my space, I'll call for his brothers!

The pyramids were vast, but what fascinated Thutmose was the head of a stone sphinx, just sticking out of the sand. He thought it must be a likeness of the god Harmachis, so he prayed that his brothers might leave him in peace.
Then, falling asleep in the shade of the great sphinx, Thutmose had the strangest dream.

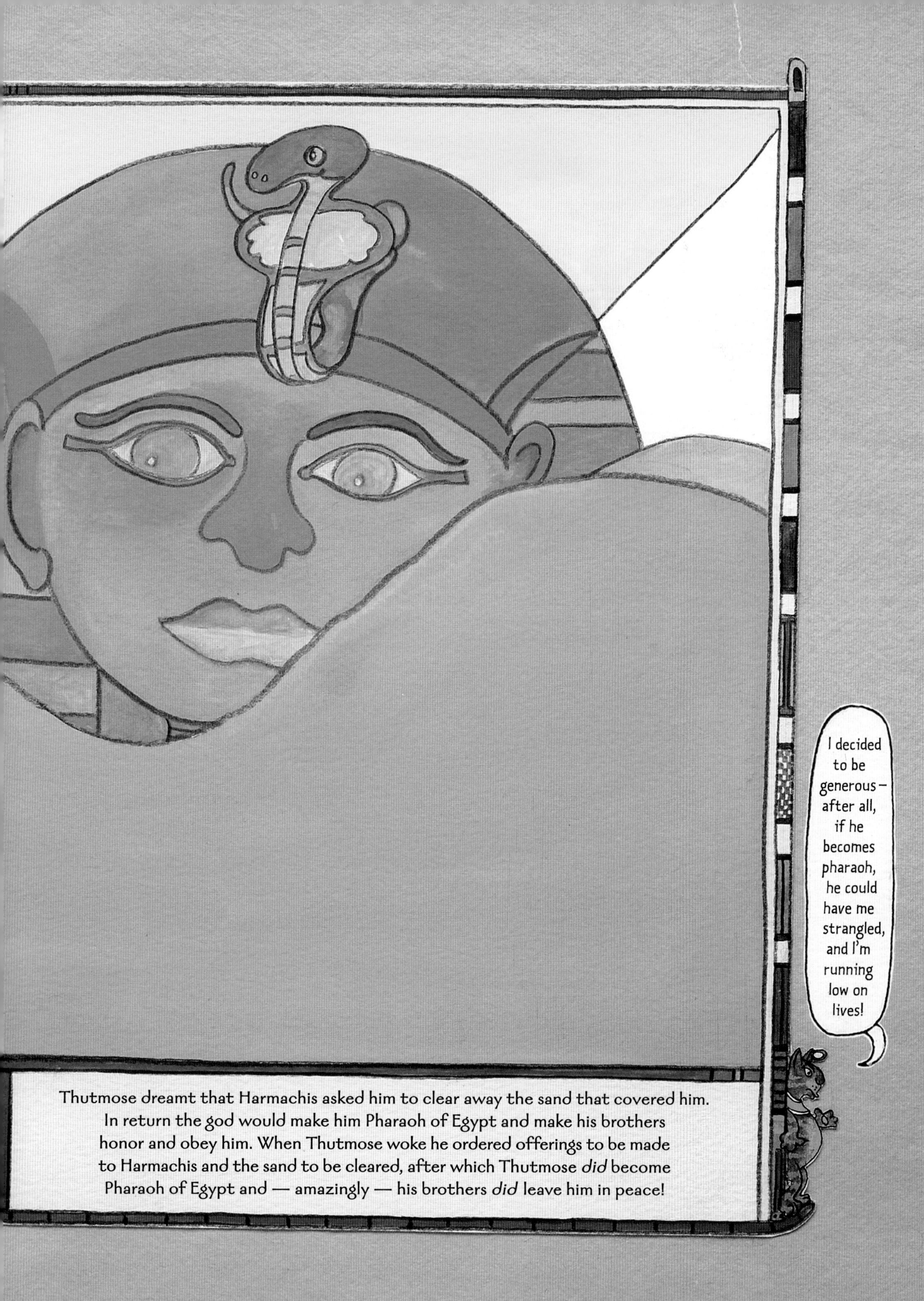

I decided to be generous – after all, if he becomes pharaoh, he could have me strangled, and I'm running low on lives!

Thutmose dreamt that Harmachis asked him to clear away the sand that covered him. In return the god would make him Pharaoh of Egypt and make his brothers honor and obey him. When Thutmose woke he ordered offerings to be made to Harmachis and the sand to be cleared, after which Thutmose *did* become Pharaoh of Egypt and — amazingly — his brothers *did* leave him in peace!

After seventy days his body was placed in a huge tomb in The Valley of the Kings. On the outside of the tomb was inscribed a terrible curse, warning all those that dared to enter the tomb not to disturb the peace of the young pharaoh.

Death shall come on swift wings to him that disturbs the peace of the king.

PHARAOH TUTANKHAMEN
All this is mine now — I can do with it what I WILL!
When Pharaoh Thutmose died, Egypt was a rich and peaceful country, but all this changed when the crown passed to his youngest brother, Akhenaten.
Aten is a minor god.
He is the ONLY god.
You'll anger the other gods.
They don't exist, and you're fired.
One god can't look after us all.
He has the power of all the gods within him!
That's not possible.
Guards, strangle the heretic, NOW!
Akhenaten showed little respect for his people's ancient beliefs. He decreed that the sun god, Aten, was the only god. He fired all Amen Ra's priests and destroyed all his shrines and temples.
Not again! This is beyond the limit.
Pharaoh, the Nubians are about to invade us.
Go away; can't you see I'm busy building a temple, for Aten?
Pharaoh Akhenaten took little interest in governing Egypt; his only interest was in building temples in honor of Aten.
Neighbor, why have you killed me for two grains of wheat?
Why not? There are no gods to anger — except Aten, and he's an imposter!
The people were confused and angry at the loss of their ancient gods, and Egypt fell into a state of disorder.
STOP! Read the opposite page before opening the flap, or be cursed forever!

Hurrah, hurrah, it's Tut for pharaoh!
So when Akhenaten died and his son, Tutankhaten, became pharaoh, they were delighted . . . even though he was a frail nine-year-old child who walked with a stick.
I wonder if Dad could have been wrong about this Aten god thing.
OOPS!
If only we were still living we would tell you that he was!
With the help of his adviser, Ay, Tutankhaten tried to uphold his dad's beliefs, but he soon saw how unhappy it made his people.
Your father will be turning in his tomb!
OOPS!
Mother, I'm eleven years old and I'll do what I want. Praise be to Ra!
So, after two years, he changed his name to Tutankh*amen* in honor of Amen Ra and reinstated the priests and temples.
So are we all friends again, and can we live in peace?
Yes, thanks to our great god, Amen Ra.
He threw lavish parties in honor of Amen Ra and gradually began to win the hearts of the old priests and his people.
Which god is going to save me now?
I warned you not to climb pyramids!
Then, when he was only nineteen years old, Tutankhamen had a fall and fractured his thigh. Frail from birth and also suffering from malaria, the young pharaoh quickly weakened and died.
You can open the flaps now; I expect you'll be cursed anyway!

Death shall come on swift wings to him that disturbs the peace of the king.

The tomb was filled with a vast feast of treasures, including 130 walking sticks, to aid Pharaoh Tutankhamen's journey to the next life. Maybe the richness of the treasures was also a way of thanking the young pharaoh for reinstating the Egyptians' ancient beliefs in their many wonderful gods.

CLEOPATRA, THE LAST PHARAOH OF EGYPT
That's me – Cleo, Queen of the Nile!
Isn't this fun, Cleo? We can both have our faces on Egyptian coins!
Just mine will do; you've got such an ugly mug.
Cleopatra was not a great beauty, but she was ambitious and very clever and she wanted to be Queen of Egypt.
This throne is too small for both of us.
You have to share!
In 51 BC, Cleopatra became joint ruler with her husband and brother, Ptolemy XIII, but she wanted the throne for herself!
I need to have a little word with Caesar... ALONE!
No chance!
When the great Roman leader Julius Caesar visited Egypt, Cleopatra decided to seek his help.
Well brother, two can play at that game.
NO ENTRY
NO ENTRY
Ptolemy realized that Cleopatra was up to no good and tried to stop her from meeting Caesar.
Gift for the mighty Caesar.
ENTER
ENTER
But Ptolemy's guards were no match for Cleopatra. She hid in a rolled carpet, which was presented to Caesar as a gift!

Pharaoh Cleo is not Egyptian; she's Macedonian Greek.
But I love Egypt!
You'd better!
Arrow, Cleo's pet leopard, is Egyptian.
Ouch!
Pharaoh Cleo loves all cats. Arrow does not.
Gulp!
Another life gone!
It may be my last.

Rid me of Ptolemy and together we can rule the world!
Anything you say, my little rug!
Trouble comes in many guises.
When the carpet was unrolled and Cleopatra popped out, Caesar was captivated and agreed to rid her of Ptolemy.
Tell all of Egypt that it's mine, all mine!
In the civil war that followed, Ptolemy was killed and Cleopatra became the sole ruler of Egypt.
He will be Emperor of Rome and Pharaoh of Egypt.
But only after us, my little rug.
Cleopatra began to think she might rule the world and went with Caesar to Rome, along with their baby, named Caesarion.
One day, I will make a beautiful corpse, but not today!
The couple's growing ambition shocked the Roman senators, and after months of plotting, they assassinated Caesar.
We must repair the canals so the fields are watered. We must trade more. We must . . .
O mighty Pharaoh, you are so wise.
Cleopatra fled back to Egypt, where she set about restoring her power and her country's wealth.

Clever Cleo speaks several languages.
I can even converse with an Egyptian.
She bathes in donkey milk to improve her skin.
Don't peek!
I drink the stuff for that sleek, furry-feline look.
Mmm, maybe that look wouldn't suit Cleo!
Rami!

With Caesar dead, Cleopatra needed another Roman ally to prevent Egypt from becoming part of the Roman Empire. So Cleopatra dressed herself as the goddess Isis and set sail for Tarsus to meet Mark Antony, one of Rome's new leaders.

Like Caesar before him, Antony immediately forgot his Roman wife and went back to Egypt
with Cleopatra. For many years Antony abandoned Rome for Cleopatra,
until finally the Roman leader Octavius declared war on them.

For months they fought, and it seemed that neither side would ever win.
Enough, let's go home.
Cleo, don't leave me.
Yes! That makes me the WINNER!
Until one day, in the midst of a sea battle, Cleopatra and her navy suddenly turned and fled, leaving Octavius triumphant.
You are now my only friend.
Antony sailed back to Egypt a broken man. Beaten in battle and betrayed by Cleopatra, he fell on his sword.
You're my prisoner and my slave!
Octavius was delighted and couldn't wait to parade Cleopatra as his slave through the streets of all the cities she had ruled.
I must return to Amen Ra.
If he'll have you!
First, I'd like to remind you of the brilliance of we ancient Egyptians.
Boring!
Around 1500 BC we invented glass making ... probably!
A glass fish
Around 1160 BC we drew the world's first known maps ... definitely!

Come, it is an honor to bite the arm of a pharaoh!
The Queen of Egypt would never submit to such a fate and managed to escape to her tomb. There she killed herself with the help of an asp whose bite, she believed, would make her immortal. Maybe she was right, for with her death Egypt became part of the Roman Empire, and so Cleopatra will always be remembered as the last of Egypt's great pharaohs.
We also wrote the first medical textbooks ... sickeningly!
Ways to remove a wart ...
Sadly, it won't save Cleo from the asp venom.
The venom of an asp is fatal.
So I'll be off. They say the gods never forget a favorite.
I'm hoping.
Farewell, or as we say:

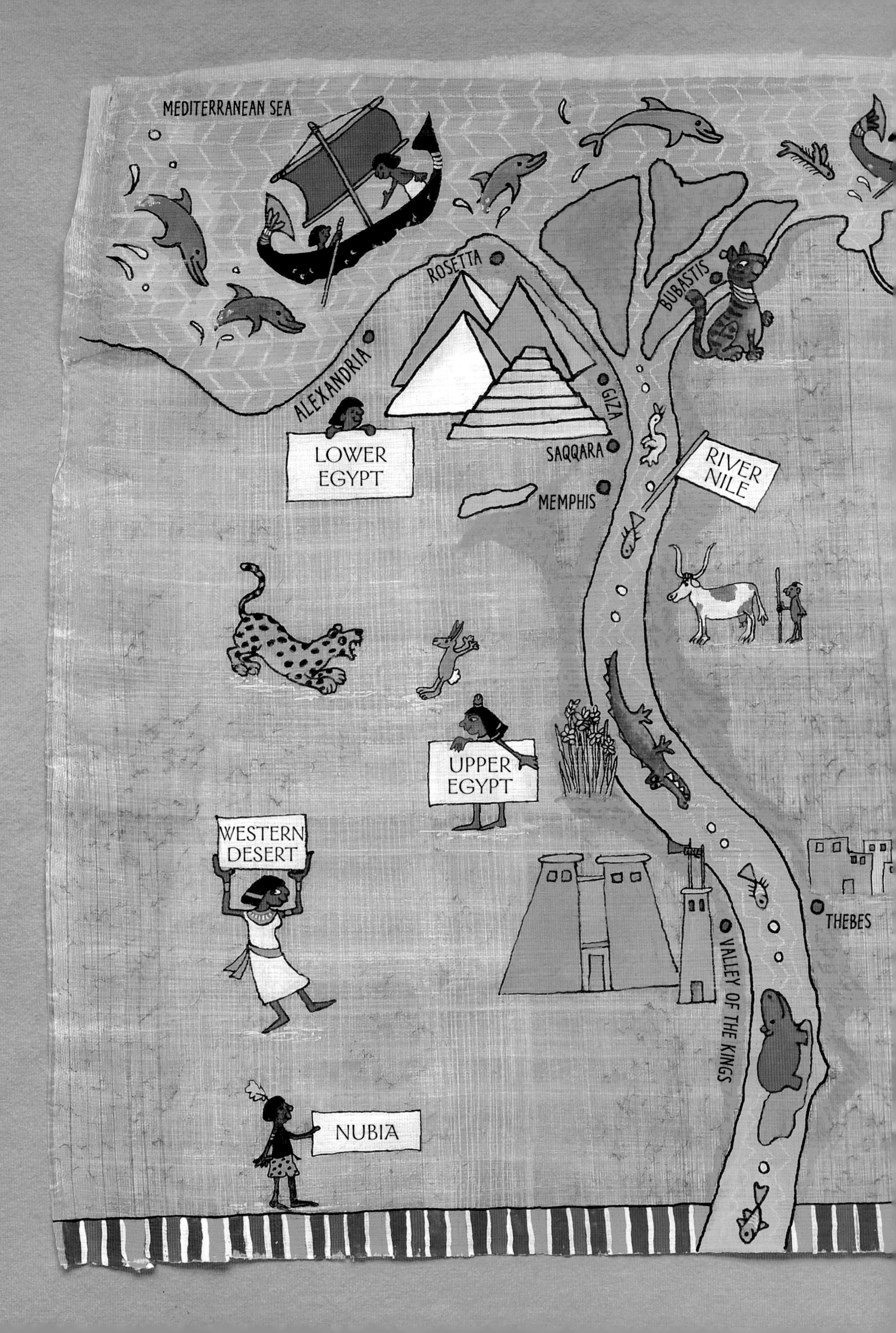

MEDITERRANEAN SEA
ROSETTA
BUBASTIS
ALEXANDRIA
GIZA
LOWER EGYPT
SAQQARA
RIVER NILE
MEMPHIS
UPPER EGYPT
WESTERN DESERT
THEBES
VALLEY OF THE KINGS
NUBIA

EASTERN
DESERT
RED
SEA

First U.S. paperback edition 2013

The Library of Congress has cataloged the hardcover edition as follows:
Williams, Marcia, date.
Ancient Egypt : tales of gods and pharaohs /
Marcia Williams.— 1st U.S. ed.
p. cm.
ISBN 978-0-7636-5308-8 (hardcover)
1. Egypt—Religion. 2. Mythology, Egyptian. I. Title.
BL2441.3.W55 2011
398.20932'022—dc22
2010040745

ISBN 978-0-7636-6315-5 (paperback)

18 19 20 APS 10 9 8 7 6 5

Printed in Humen, Dongguan, China

This book was typeset in Galahad and Kosmik.
The illustrations were done in gouache and ink.

Candlewick Press
99 Dover Street
Somerville, Massachusetts 02144

visit us at www.candlewick.com

It has come from beginning to end.
Miw!

Marcia Williams has written and illustrated many books in her highly successful and entertaining comic-strip style. Among her many retellings are *Chaucer's Canterbury Tales*, *Charles Dickens and Friends*, and *Tales from Shakespeare*. About *Ancient Egypt*, she says, "The ancient Egyptians were among the very first comic-strip artists, which is one of the reasons why I enjoy their art and history so much. The tales collected here include many of my favorites — they have that inspiring mixture of the weird and wonderful — and centuries on they remain among the greatest stories ever told. I hope you enjoy them and that they become your favorites too!" Marcia Williams lives in London.